In the War

The Blitz

Simon Adams

WAYLAND

First published in 2008 by Wayland

Copyright © Wayland 2008

Wayland
338 Euston Road
London NW1 3BH

Wayland Australia
Level 17/207 Kent Street
Sydney, NSW 2000

Editor: Camilla Lloyd
Designer: Phipps Design
Picture researcher: Shelley Noronha

Picture Acknowledgments: The author and publisher would like to thank the following for their pictures
to be reproduced in this publication: Cover photograph: Wayland Picture Library, Topfoto (front);
© Bettmann/Corbis: 11, 21, 22, Corbis: 5, 26, Hulton-Deutsch Collection/Corbis: 10, 18, 19, 25, 29;
Peter Hicks: 7; Topfoto: 9, 12, 16, 20, 23, 27, 28; Wayland Picture Library: 1, 4, 6, 8, 13, 14, 15, 17, 24.

British Library Cataloguing in Publication Data:
Adams, Simon, 1955-
    The Blitz. - (In the war)
    World War, 1939-1945 - Campaigns - Great Britain – Juvenile literature
    2. World War, 1939-1945 – Aerial operations, German - Juvenile literature
    3. London(England) - History - Bombardment, 1940-1941 - Juvenile literature
    I. Title
    940.5'4211

ISBN: 978 0 7502 5350 5

Printed in China

Wayland is a division of Hachette Children's Books, an Hachette Livre UK company
www.hachettelivre.co.uk

Contents

World War II

The Blitz was the bombardment of British towns and cities carried out by the Germans during World War II. The war had started in September 1939 and lasted until 1945. The immediate cause of the war was Germany's invasion of Poland. Poland's **allies**, Britain and France, then declared war on Germany.

In 1918, Germany had been defeated at the end of World War I. The peace terms it had to sign were harsh. It lost much territory and had to pay massive **compensation** to Britain, France, and the other victorious allies. In 1933, Adolf Hitler and the Nazi Party came to power in Germany. Hitler wanted to overthrow the peace terms and make Germany a powerful country again.

People learned that war had been declared from newspapers and the radio.

Think about

What sort of thoughts would you have had on the day war was declared?

NEWS
OF THE
WORLD
WAR
DECLARED
(OFFICIAL)

Hitler quickly built up Germany's armed services and tore up her international agreements. He took over Austria in 1938 and, later the same year, seized German-speaking border areas in Czechoslovakia, occupying the country the following year. Hitler then turned his attention to Poland, demanding that it hand over the strip of Polish land that separated the main part of Germany from its eastern province of Prussia. When Poland refused, Germany invaded.

Although Britain had declared war on Germany, many people did not want to fight. They remembered the horrors of World War I and did not want to repeat them. Many people, including the prime minister, had hoped that Hitler might be bought off and were let down when this did not happen. No one wanted the war, and no one really knew what sort of war to expect.

INSIDE STORY:

'*This morning the British ambassador in Berlin handed the German government a final note, stating that unless the British government heard from them by 11 o'clock that they were prepared to withdraw their troops from Poland,* a state of war would exist between us. I have to tell you that no such undertaking has been received, and that consequently this country is at war with Germany.'

Prime Minister Neville Chamberlain made a radio broadcast to the British people on Sunday morning, 3 September.

The official declaration of war was made from the steps of the Royal Exchange in London.

Preparations for war

In 1939, Britain had a large army to defeat the Germans on land, and a powerful navy to protect the country from invasion by sea, but the British government was most frightened of attack from enemy **bombers** in the air.

A bomber could bring death and destruction to **civilian** populations. Although the British government had built up the Royal Air Force (**RAF**), many people believed that the bomber was unstoppable and would kill thousands.

INSIDE STORY:

'I think it is well ... for the man in the street to realise that there is no power on earth that can prevent him from being bombed. Whatever people may tell him, the bomber will always get through.'

Stanley Baldwin MP and a former prime minister, November 1931.

Gas masks were made for even the smallest children.

The government feared that the Germans would use poison gas, so it distributed 38 million gas masks to civilians. People were encouraged to build their own bomb shelters or to convert their cellars into shelters. Anderson shelters – named after the Home Secretary Sir John Anderson – were given free to poor families. Shelters consisted of iron sheets bolted together and placed in the backyard or garden. The shelters were then covered with soil, which some people used to grow vegetables in.

People protected homes by piling sandbags up against doors and walls to absorb a bomb's blast and putting tape on their windows to stop them shattering. **Blackouts** were enforced every night so that there were no lights to direct enemy bombers to the town below. Doors and windows were covered with thick curtains to keep the light inside, streetlights were switched off, public buildings blacked out, and buses and cars drove with masked headlights. Most importantly, sirens warning of an air-raid were placed in every town and district. When people heard the sirens go off, they knew an air-raid was about to begin.

An Anderson shelter protected people from bombs but could also be used to grow vegetables.

Think about
How do you think you would prepare yourself for war?

The Battle of Britain

Within minutes of war being declared on 3 September 1939, air-raid sirens sounded across Britain. In fact the siren was a false alarm and no raid took place that day.

The first few months of the war were so quiet that people called it a 'Phoney War'. Germany conquered far-away Poland in September, and war broke out in Finland that winter. Britain, however, remained untouched. Children were **evacuated** from the cities – some were sent abroad to Canada or the USA – in case they were bombed, but many returned home when the **bombs** failed to drop.

This changed in April 1940, when Germany invaded Denmark and Norway. The British prime minister Neville Chamberlain resigned on 10 May and was replaced by Winston Churchill, who formed a government of all political parties. That same day, German troops invaded Holland, Belgium and France. When the French made peace at the end of June, Britain stood alone against Germany.

Children were evacuated out of towns and cities and sent to safety in the countryside.

In July, the Battle of Britain began. Hitler planned Operation Sea Lion to invade Britain but needed first to clear the RAF from the skies. The first attacks by the **Luftwaffe** (German Air Force) were directed at Channel ports and shipping. When these failed to force a decisive battle with the RAF, the *Luftwaffe* turned its attention to attacking aircraft and airfields. The battle raged in the skies over southern England for three months.

Although the German pilots had more experience, the two sides were well matched in pilot training and the quality of fighter aircraft. The British, however, fought well over their own land and used **radar** and intelligence information to warn them of enemy attacks.

By early October, the British pilots had won, causing the invasion of Britain to be postponed. The Blitz, however, was about to begin.

Think about

How might you have felt if you were a pilot in the Battle of Britain?

A German Messerschmitt fighter chases a British Spitfire during the Battle of Britain.

The Blitz begins

In September, the Germans turned their attention to bombing British cities to destruction, hoping that the British people would then surrender. The British called these attacks the Blitz.

The world 'Blitz' comes from the German word *blitzkrieg*, meaning 'lightning war', in which tanks, aircraft and motorized infantry combine to attack the enemy at speed and break up the mass of its troops into small, easily attacked groups. The British applied this term to describe air-raids on London and other British cities, shortening the word to just 'blitz'.

Ports and airfields had been bombed during the Battle of Britain, and the centre of London was bombed quite heavily on 24 August.

INSIDE STORY:

'For Londoners, there are no such things as good nights; there are only bad nights, worse nights and better nights. Hardly anyone has slept at all in the last week. ... On all sides one hears the grim phrase "We shall get used to it."'

Mollie Panter-Downes was an English woman who sent a regular report to the *New Yorker* magazine in the USA (14 September 1940).

Two German Dornier bombers fly over London's East End during the Blitz as fires rage below them.

On the afternoon of 7 September 1940, the scale of these attacks increased when a massive air-raid took place against London. The Blitz had now begun.

Huge fires broke out in the East End that could be seen across London, and many buildings were completely destroyed. That day 430 civilians were killed and more than 1,600 seriously injured. Thousands were made homeless. The German bombers returned the next night, killing 400 civilians. The following night, 370 people were killed. The raids continued every night for 76 nights in succession, except when bad weather called a halt on 2 November.

The raids caused massive destruction. Factories, warehouses, offices and shops were destroyed, schools and hospitals wrecked, and entire streets of houses burned down. Famous London landmarks, like old churches, disappeared forever.

Many houses were completely destroyed by the bombs during the Blitz.

Think about
Would you get used to nightly bombing?

Raiders overhead!

In 1937, the British government estimated that bombing raids would start as soon as war broke out and kill 600,000 people, and injure twice that number, within two months. It planned **Air-Raid Precautions** (**ARPs**), such as providing shelters and organizing a blackout, and recruited 200,000 people by mid-1938 to act as ARP wardens.

There were roughly ten wardens for every square mile of a city or town; there were fewer in rural areas. Almost all were part-timers coming on duty once they had finished work for the day. About one-sixth were women. Once the red alert – 'Raiders overhead!' – sounded and the siren, nicknamed 'Wailing Willie' or 'Wailing Winnie' because of its funny noise, wailed out across the town, the ARP wardens were in charge.

The warden's first duty was to direct people to the shelters, urging the slower ones to hurry and helping those who were old or ill. Wardens were chosen for their knowledge of the local area and its people. They knew who lived where, who had been evacuated, and where extra people were staying. They listed all this information and ticked everyone's name off the list as they flooded into the shelters. If someone was missing, the warden ran round to their house to check up on them.

An ARP warden rescues a young girl from a bombed building.

Think about
Do you think you could have been an ARP warden?

Once the bombs started dropping, the wardens stayed above ground. They checked the damage at every bombsite and used their local knowledge to direct the emergency services to where survivors might be buried. They also checked local shelters to make sure people were safe, and gave them news of what was happening. When the 'All clear' siren sounded, the wardens could relax, although they would be back on duty the next night.

The Women's Voluntary Service (WVS) ran mobile canteens to provide food and drink for ARP wardens and emergency service workers during the Blitz.

INSIDE STORY:

Barbara Nixon was a full-time ARP warden in Finsbury, London. She soon realised she needed to learn everything from *'the names of the residents in each house, and which shelter they used, [fire] hydrants, cul-de-sacs [dead-end streets], danger points in the area, to the whereabouts of the old and infirm [ill] who would need help in getting to shelter, telephone numbers and the addresses of rest centres.'*

Going underground

During an air-raid, the German bombers dropped **incendiary bombs** and conventional high-explosive bombs, setting light to or blowing up buildings and causing them to crash down into the street. The safest place for people to be during a raid was in an underground shelter.

Some people were lucky enough to have cellars under their houses they could shelter in. Others took shelter under the stairs. Most people, however, made use of the various public shelters that were quickly brought in to use.

Think about
What would you have been thinking about while in the shelter?

A bedtime story helped children get to sleep each night in their shelters.

'Public Shelter' notices appeared outside town halls, railway stations, offices and shops. Church crypts were rapidly converted to accommodate people overnight, as were vaults, basements and other underground rooms. Even caves were brought in to use. Shelters were also dug in public parks and commons. These muddy holes were lined with timber or concrete and furnished with stairs, seats and primitive sanitation. Some were built of bricks.

For most people, the nearest shelter was their own Anderson shelter in their backyard or garden (see page 7). About 1.5 million of these had been delivered free to poor families earning less than £250 a year – the government thought this number should be enough for up to 6 million people to use – and 50,000 more were produced each week. However, there were still not enough to go round, and the shelters had yet to go on sale to those rich enough to buy them. Many of the shelters that had been given out had not been properly built, as it required considerable skill and strength to construct a shelter properly from the kit.

There wasn't much space through which to climb down into an Anderson shelter.

INSIDE STORY:

'He'd painted the inside of the shelter white and he'd got butterflies painted on the walls. He had a little stove down there; it was a real little home from home. … As soon as we'd had our evening meal we'd go down there with our books and knitting, whatever we were doing.'

Gwendolen Watts remembers her father's Anderson shelter in Birmingham.

The tube

The most obvious place for Londoners to shelter during the Blitz was the underground railway system – the **tube**. However, the government refused to open the tunnels up, as it wanted to keep the underground running to get people out of the city and home before the evening air-raids and to evacuate any casualties.

On 'Black Saturday', 7 September 1940, the start of the Blitz, some Londoners ignored the ban and forced their way past soldiers and into the underground at Liverpool Street Station. The government then agreed to open the underground up, 'insofar as it does not interfere with the transport of London's workers.'

Although only about four or five per cent of London's total population sheltered in the underground, this still meant that 177,000 people used it as their nightly shelter. Conditions at first were poor, as people had to lie on the platforms.

Aldwych tube station in London was closed to trains and turned into a permanent underground shelter.

INSIDE STORY:

'It took me a quarter of an hour to get from the station entrance to the platform. Even in the darkened booking hall I stumbled over huddled bodies ... Going down the stairs I saw mothers feeding infants. Little boys and girls lay across their parents' bodies because there was no room on the winding stairs.'

A *South London Press* reporter visited the Elephant and Castle tube station on 1 October 1940.

By March 1941, bunk beds were built in most of the 76 underground stations in use and chemical toilets installed. Some old stations and tunnels were brought back into use. People made their own entertainment, singing songs or playing cards.

The underground was not always the safest place to be. Balham Station took a direct hit on 14 October 1940, killing or burying alive 63 people. About 1,500 people rushed to Bethnal Green station after the alert sounded at 8.17 pm on 3 March 1943. The station was still being built and a woman carrying her baby tripped and fell down narrow stairs. Within seconds, people fell on top of her and were crushed to death. In all, 173 people died, 62 of them children, making up a third of all wartime deaths in the area.

Think about
Have you travelled on the tube recently? What would it have been like to live there during the Blitz?

There wasn't much room to sleep on a tube platform, but it was much safer underground than on the surface.

Blitz children

Growing up in London or another big city during the Blitz was a very scary experience. Some children had been evacuated from the cities into the safer areas of the countryside before the Blitz started but many remained behind. They often did not understand what was happening and why bombs kept dropping around them.

Many had never seen an enemy bomber before and at first thought the planes flying overhead were British. However, children soon became expert plane spotters. They learned to identify the different wing shapes and markings, and the distinct engine noise of each type. They also quickly identified the different types of bomb, collecting pieces of **shrapnel** and parts of German planes that crashed during a raid.

Fancy dress parties and other entertainments were provided for children sheltering from the Blitz.

The first bomb attack was often the worst, but, like everyone else, children soon learned to cope with the raids. They made themselves at home in the shelters, sometimes made new friends, and carried on with life as normally as possible. School continued each day, although often in temporary accommodation. Buses and tubes still ran, and friends still met up on street corners to kick a football around or tell each other stories of last night's raid.

Not every raid ended well. Thousands of children were killed or wounded in the raids, while many lost friends and family. Others lost their fathers, who were killed while fighting overseas or sailing across the North Atlantic in the convoys of ships bringing military supplies and food to Britain. Children also lost their homes, toys and clothes. Above all, they lost their normal childhood, for growing up in the Blitz was like no other childhood in history.

INSIDE STORY:

'A bomb fell in our back garden and I must say I was scared stiff. We stayed where we were and everything seemed to be falling in on us. ... The road was full of rescue workers and I saw a friend of mine carried by a blanket and the blanket was over her head and I knew she was dead.'

Isabel Kiernan was a teenager in Liverpool during the Blitz. She remembers the day her house was bombed.

The British prime minister Winston Churchill, the German leader Adolf Hitler and the Italian leader Benito Mussolini replace Punch and Judy in this special wartime version of the puppet show.

Think about
Imagine if your friends were killed, or you lost your house. How would you feel?

Fighting the flames

One of the main dangers during the Blitz was fire. Incendiary bombs set buildings alight, while high-explosive bombs ripped them apart, breaking gas mains and causing explosions that engulfed the building. Some nights, so many buildings in the cities were on fire that it was almost as bright as daylight.

The ARP wardens were the first to spot a fire. They tried to put out small fires themselves with water pumps, sandbags or shovels of earth, and they dropped small incendiary bombs into buckets of water to smother them. If the fire quickly spread throughout a building, they called the fire and other emergency services. When the fire brigade arrived, the ARP warden told them where the nearest mains water tap was, and soon they would be aiming their fire hoses at the blaze. Sometimes this meant climbing up extendable ladders and fighting the blaze from above.

Emergency services pumped water from rivers and docks to fight large fires in warehouses and factories bombed during the Blitz.

While the fire fighters tackled the fire, the Heavy Rescue Squad swung into action to move **masonry** and debris to rescue those trapped inside buildings.

Think about
What would it have been like to be a fire fighter in the Blitz?

Gas, water and electricity supplies were quickly cut off, but often too late for the many people who had survived the collapse of their building only to drown or be gassed, as masks offered no protection against gas from homes. Stretcher parties arrived to help the wounded, or carry them to first aid posts or to ambulances that took them to hospital.

The pressure on the rescue services was immense. They had to fight far more fires each night than they could possibly respond to. They had to decide which buildings would have the most survivors and which should be left to burn out.

INSIDE STORY:

'We went up to the roof to look. At Shepherd's Bush flames were leaping, and towards the City they were gigantic. As I walked up the road I could see the smoke. A great red glow filled the sky – I had no need of a torch – I could see every step I took and could have read a book if I had wished.'

Mrs Vere Hodgson was a welfare worker in west London and kept a diary during the Blitz. She recorded a raid on London on 30 December 1940.

St Paul's Cathedral remained undamaged during the Blitz despite the heavy bombing of London.

All clear!

There was no more welcome sound after hours of bombing than the 'All clear' siren. The siren was sounded after the RAF's early warning radar systems in airports around southern England declared the area free of incoming bombers. The night's raid was over. Now the horrors of the day awaited survivors.

Gradually people left their shelters and returned home. Some found their homes undamaged, others found a smouldering ruin. Fires still burned in many places and the rubble of damaged and destroyed buildings was left across the streets. Gas, water and electricity supplies had often been cut and telephone cables brought down.

Most urgently of all, people left the shelters anxious to find out if their family and friends had survived the raid. Each night brought a new death toll.

Milk, post and other deliveries continued as usual during the Blitz.

Think about
What would you expect to see after an air-raid?

Members of the Women's Voluntary Service (WVS) worked alongside the ARP wardens, breaking the bad news to those whose homes had been destroyed and sometimes taking relatives to the mortuary to identify the dead.

One of the worst after-effects of a raid was an unexploded bomb. Most high-explosive bombs blew up on impact, but one in ten did not, usually because of a mechanical or electrical fault. When such a bomb was found, buildings had to be evacuated again, streets closed off and people moved away until bomb-disposal units turned up to make them safe. Many such bombs lay deep in the ground, making it very difficult to disarm them, while others were never found. By the end of 1940, at least 3,000 unexploded bombs were still waiting to be defused in London alone. Unexploded bombs are still being found today.

INSIDE STORY:

Dorothy Barton worked in London during the Blitz. The morning after one of the biggest raids on the city – on 29 December 1940 – she crossed London Bridge and went to work. When she reached her office, she found it the only one still standing in the street.

'Suddenly a policeman rushed in [to the office] and said, "Everyone out, there's an exploded bomb in the backyard." I made my way to the end of the street again.'

A grandmother and her family look at the wreckage of their Liverpool home bombed during the Blitz.

Out of London

The Blitz did not just affect London. Every major town and city in Britain was bombed, often many times, with huge loss of life and damage to houses, factories and other buildings. Many of the places bombed were major military or industrial centres, containing ports, **munitions** and aircraft factories and other targets. Inevitably, however, thousands of homes were bombed as well and many civilians lost their lives.

The scale of these raids was huge. Between the start of the Blitz in September 1940 and the end of the year, London was raided 126 times, Liverpool 60 times, Birmingham 36 times and Coventry 21 times. One of the worst affected was Coventry. The city was a centre of aircraft manufacture and other war industries and had already suffered 17 attacks by the time the big raid happened on the night of 14/15 November. That night, bombers dropped 500 tons of high explosives and 30,000 incendiaries, killing at least 568 people and badly injuring more than 1,200 people.

INSIDE STORY:

'The centre of the town is roped off and no one is allowed within half a mile of it,' one Coventry woman reported. *'There are so many unexploded bombs about, they are talking of blasting the town because none of the buildings are safe ... one can't get near the Council House for people waiting for death certificates ... we are indeed a stricken city.'*

Plymouth was just one of the many British cities bombed heavily during the Blitz.

The city centre was destroyed, including the historic old cathedral. One in twelve houses were totally destroyed and two-thirds seriously damaged, and one-third of all factories were wrecked.

The death toll in Coventry would have been far worse had not thousands of people trekked out of the city every night to seek shelter in nearby small towns and villages. As it was, the 79 public shelters and numerous Anderson shelters and basement cellars protected most people who remained in the city. The raid was so bad it gave a new word to both the German and English languages: *Koventrieren*, 'to Coventrate', or lay waste by aerial bombardment.

Think about
How would you respond if your town or city was totally destroyed in a raid?

The ancient cathedral of Coventry was totally destroyed by German bombs during a massive air-raid on the city.

The Baby Blitz

London received its biggest ever raid on 10/11 May 1941, with 1,436 people killed and 1,792 seriously injured. Belfast was 'Coventrated' and Clydebank near Glasgow was so badly hit on 13/14 March that all but seven of its 12,000 houses were damaged!

In June 1941, Hitler turned his attention east and invaded the **USSR** but the bombing in Britain did not stop for good. By now the RAF was raiding German towns, destroying the ancient city of Lübeck in March 1942. In response, the German Press and Information Division announced that British targets would be drawn from the Baedeker guidebook *Great Britain: Handbook for Travellers*: 'We shall go out to bomb every building in Britain marked with three stars in the Guide.' The so-called Baedeker raids of April to June 1942 hit old towns such as Bath and York, killing 16,000 people.

When a V-2 rocket hit Smithfield meat market in London in March 1945, 115 people were killed and hundreds injured.

Think about

Can you imagine living through more than four years of bombing?

Raids continued into 1943, but the tide of the war was now turning in Britain's favour. However, the *Luftwaffe* returned for a second 'Baby' or 'Little' Blitz in January 1944. By now a new type of shelter was being built. Named after the Home Secretary, Herbert Morrison, the Morrison shelter consisted of a rectangular steel cage 2 m (6ft 6 in) long, standing 85 cm (33 in) off the ground and could fit two adults and two small children lying down. Its great advantage was that it fitted inside a house.

The Baby Blitz ended in April 1944. The Germans still had two further weapons to use. Some 2,500 V-1 'flying bombs' landed in southern England after June, followed in September by 518 more powerful V-2 rockets. Almost 9,000 people were killed and more than 24,000 were seriously injured. Only with the end of the war in May 1945 did the Blitz finally come to an end.

INSIDE STORY:

'*We eke out the sitting room fire with chunks of wood from the bombed buildings now. … At the moment we are burning pieces of Buckingham Mansions, which gives me a sinking feeling for, at this very moment, Buckingham Mansions might quite easily be burning a piece of us!*'

Gladys Cox remembered the Baby Blitz in north London.

This woman's house in southern England was totally destroyed by a flying V-1 bomb.

The end of the war

The end of the war in Europe in May 1945, followed by the end of the war against Japan in August 1945, brought peace to the weary people of Britain. They had endured six years of fighting, but they had also experienced five years of bombing and their losses were large.

In total, about 60,000 civilians lost their lives during the Blitz. About half of those lived in London. More than 85,000 people went to hospital with serious injuries, while a further 150,000 were slightly injured. Half a million houses were totally destroyed and four million more were seriously damaged. There was also huge destruction to schools, hospitals, public buildings, factories, railways and roads. Many famous cities were flattened, and old buildings lost forever.

A jubilant newspaper seller announces the end of the war.

Formal recognition of the bravery shown by men and women during the Blitz was made on 23 September 1940. King George VI broadcast from Buckingham Palace to announce 'a new mark of honour' named after England's patron saint, St George. The George Cross was the civilian equivalent of the Victoria Cross and was awarded for extreme bravery; the George Medal was awarded for 'good conduct and valour', in Churchill's words.

King George VI and Queen Elizabeth stayed in London during the Blitz and did much to raise morale among the civilian population.

The Germans planned to bomb Britain into surrender during the Blitz. They thought that the British people would lose the will to fight and make peace with Germany to end the bombing. This did not happen, any more than British bombing raids on Germany made the German people surrender. When faced with bombing raids night after night, people stuck together and helped each other out in what some people call the 'Blitz spirit'. The Blitz did not affect who won the war, but it changed many peoples' lives forever.

Think about

The Blitz ended more than 60 years ago. Do you think it would be different if it happened today?

Timeline

3 September 1939	Germany invades Poland at the start of World War II.
10 May 1940	Winston Churchill becomes prime minister; Germany invades the Low Countries and France.
22 June 1940	France surrenders to Germany; Britain fights Germany alone.
10 July–12 October 1940	Battle of Britain is fought between the RAF and *Luftwaffe* for the control of British skies.
7 September 1940	The Blitz begins when German bombers raid London.
14/15 November 1940	Major raid on Coventry.
10/11 May 1941	London endures its worst ever raid; the Blitz ends, although raids continue into 1943.
22 June 1941	Germany invades USSR, which joins the war on the British side.
7 December 1941	Japan attacks US forces at Pearl Harbor; USA joins the war on the Allied side, turning it into a truly world war.
28/29 March 1942	British bombers devastate German city of Lübeck.
23 April–6 June 1942	Baedeker raids against historic British cities.
21 January–19 April 1944	The Baby Blitz.
6 June 1944	Allied troops land in Normandy, France on D-Day.
13 June 1944–29 March 1945	V-1 missile attacks on London and the southeast.
8 September 1944–27 March 1945	V-2 rocket attacks on London.
8 May 1945	VE Day celebrates end of the war in Europe.

Glossary

Air-Raid Precautions (ARP) Measures taken to protect people and buildings against air-raids.

Allies Countries linked to each other by a treaty of friendship.

Blackout The hiding or extinguishing of all artificial light at night, especially in a city, that might be visible to enemy aircraft during an air-raid.

Bomb Hollow shell containing an explosive, incendiary or other destructive substance.

Bomber Military aircraft specially built to carry and drop bombs on an enemy target.

Civilian A person whose work or family is mainly civil rather than military.

Compensation Money paid to a country (or a person) for loss or injury.

Evacuated When people were moved from danger to a place of relative safety.

Incendiary bomb Bomb designed to start fires.

Luftwaffe German Air Force.

Masonry Stone and brick work.

Munitions Military equipment and stores, especially ammunition such as bullets, bombs and grenades.

Radar High-frequency radio pulse transmitted and reflected back by the object indicating its location, used to detect enemy airplanes in the sky.

RAF Britain's Royal Air Force.

Shrapnel Metal fragment of a bomb.

Tube, the Common nickname for London Underground, because of its tube-shaped train tunnels.

USSR Union of Soviet Socialist Republics, a former country now known as Russia.

Further information

Books to read

In the War: Evacuation by Simon Adams (Wayland, 2008)

In the War: Food and Rations by Peter Hicks (Wayland, 2008)

In the War: School Life by Peter Hicks (Wayland, 2008)

World War Two: The Home Front by Ann Kramer (Franklin Watts, 2006)

World War Two: Causes, Course and Consequences by Simon Adams (Franklin Watts, 2005)

World War Two: Woman and War by Ann Kramer (Franklin Watts, 2005)

Eyewitness World War II by Simon Adams (Dorling Kindersley, 2004))

Websites

http://www.bbc.co.uk/history/worldwars/wwtwo
BBC history site on WWII.

www.worldwar2exraf.co.uk/Online%20Museum/ Museum%20Docs/Theblitz.html
Detailed site on the Blitz.

Note to parents and teachers: Every effort has been made by the publishers to ensure that these websites are suitable for children. However, because of the nature of the Internet, it is impossible to guarantee that the contents of these sites will not be altered. We strongly advise that Internet access is supervised by a responsible adult.

Index

Numbers in **bold** refer to pictures and captions.